The Rosetta Stone

and the Secret of Hieroglyphics

by Ellen B. Cutler

PEARSON

Scott
Foresman

Editorial Offices: Glenview, Illinois • Parsippany, New Jersey • New York, New York
Sales Offices: Needham, Massachusetts • Duluth, Georgia • Glenview, Illinois
Coppell, Texas • Ontario, California • Mesa, Arizona

Opener: ©DK Images; 1 ©DK Images; 3 ©DK Images; 4 Art Resource, NY; 6 ©DK Images; 8 ©DK Images; 9 ©DK Images; 10 ©DK Images; 12 ©DK Images; 15 ©DK Images

ISBN: 0-328-13466-X

6 7 8 9 10 V0G1 14 13 12 11 10 09 08 07

A Discovery

The year was 1799. France was at war with England. Soldiers were hard at work in the hot sun building a fort. The soldiers had traveled far from their homes in France to work in Rosetta, Egypt. Rosetta is located where the western Nile River Delta meets the Mediterranean Sea.

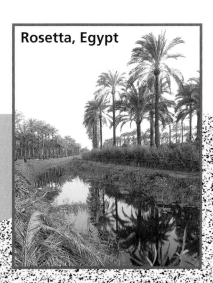

Rosetta, Egypt

MEDITERRANEAN SEA

Rosetta

NILE RIVER

EGYPT

The conflict between France and England had spread all the way to Egypt. General Napoleon Bonaparte brought his French soldiers to this country. He wanted to take over the land. He also brought painters, scientists, and **scholars** with him. These people would study Egyptian art, history, and language. Bonaparte was interested in learning about Egyptian culture as well.

Bonaparte's troops dug through the sand in search of stone that they could use to build a fort. They came upon an unusual piece of rock. It was a piece of black basalt. The edges were broken. It was clear that this long slab of stone had once been used as a marker or a sign.

The slab had three wide bands of writing. The writing on the top band was Egyptian hieroglyphics.

This was a kind of picture writing that no one knew how to read anymore. The text in the middle was written in demotic script. Demotic script was a simplified form of hieroglyphics. A few people were able to understand some of this writing. The bottom band was written in ancient Greek, a language known to many scholars.

General Napoleon Bonaparte's troops at the Battle of Aboukir Bay in Egypt

6

The Stone

The stone the troops discovered is known as the Rosetta Stone. The discovery of the Rosetta Stone made people excited all around the world. It would be a clue to figuring out the lost language of the **ancient** Egyptians. It was clear to scholars, or people who have much knowledge, that all three bands were inscribed, or written, with the same message. For a long time people had struggled to understand hieroglyphics—the script that combined letters and pictures. The Rosetta Stone would help them make sense of this ancient form of writing.

Scholars knew they could **translate** the hieroglyphic text by comparing it to the demotic script and the ancient Greek writing. The words they know would be the **link** to the unknown ones. Scholars would use the Greek text that they knew and understood to help them read the demotic script. The demotic script would help them **uncover** the meaning of the ancient Egyptian hieroglyphs. Knowing how to read hieroglyphics would help scholars learn more about the Egyptian civilization.

The Rosetta Stone

Egyptian Culture

The ancient civilization of Egypt grew up along the banks of the Nile River. Water flooded over the riverbanks every year. This left behind a rich, deep soil that allowed all kinds of crops to grow. Wide deserts on the east and the west protected Egypt from its opponents. Egypt also had a long seacoast with harbors. Egyptians sailed to distant lands and traded goods. They built beautiful **temples.** The country grew rich.

Inside an Egyptian temple

Various wars brought Egypt under Persian, Greek, and then Roman control. In 30 B.C., Egypt became part of the Roman Empire. By this time only a few priests still knew and used hieroglyphics. Fewer people used this ancient form of writing as time went on, because other forms of writing were easier to use. Slowly, the writing system was lost. No one could read or write hieroglyphics. Over time they had forgotten how.

Egyptian mummy case

The Ancient Writing

Glyph	Sound
⬜	p
⌂	t
🐇	l

The hieroglyphics system had developed in Egypt soon after 3000 B.C. The symbols, or glyphs, used in the writing changed very little over the next twenty-six hundred years.

There are between seven hundred and eight hundred symbols in Egyptian hieroglyphics. Compare that to the twenty-six letters in the English alphabet! Some of the Egyptian symbols stand for sounds. Other symbols stand for objects or ideas.

The ancient Egyptians believed that writing made words and ideas live forever. They called hieroglyphics the "language of the gods." Priests used hieroglyphics to decorate the walls of their temples with prayers and stories. Sometimes hieroglyphics were carved on wooden objects such as furniture or on jewelry.

Hieroglyphics on an Egyptian stamp

10

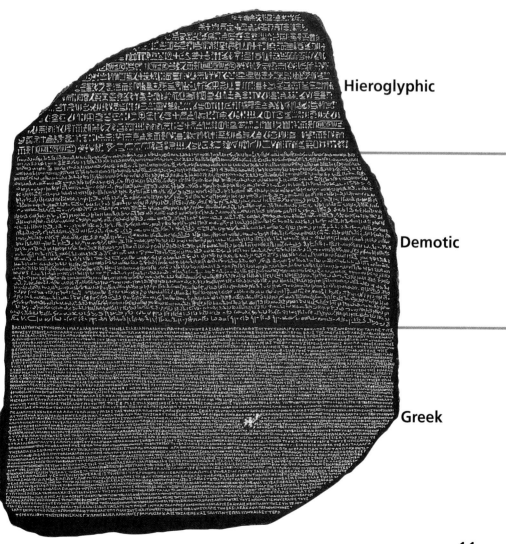

Hieroglyphics were difficult to learn and took a long time to write out, even for the ancient Egyptians. Also, the Egyptians invented a form of writing called hieratic script that was easier to use. Later this became demotic script that was even easier to write.

Hieroglyphic

Demotic

Greek

11

Finding the Key

Copies of the Rosetta Stone texts were sent to scholars all around Europe. Reading the hieroglyphics was difficult for scholars. Figuring out the meaning of each glyph was hard, slow work.

Everyone had a different idea about how to uncover the meaning. Was every symbol a picture that had a specific meaning? What did the squiggles and squares and other shapes mean? Were they meant to be read from left to right, from right to left, up and down?

It took people years to learn to read hieroglyphics. They had to do more than compare the three different forms of writing on the Rosetta Stone. They also compared the hieroglyphics on the stone to those they found on temple walls and sculptures in Egypt.

One thing they discovered was that a cartouche was a line of hieroglyphics enclosed in an oval shape. The cartouche stood for a person's name. Some of the first glyphs to be translated were the ones used for the names of kings and queens.

Cartouches on the outside wall of an Egyptian temple

Most of the credit for figuring out hieroglyphics belongs to a French man named Jean-François Champollion. He lived from 1790 to 1832.

Champollion was a **seeker** of knowledge. He was good at learning languages. He was also interested in Egyptian culture. His family told him to pursue his interests. Champollion decided that one day he would learn to read hieroglyphics.

Finally, Champollion found **triumph.** All of the time he had spent studying Egypt helped him to figure out sounds and whole ideas. Champollion had found the key to unlocking hieroglyphics.

French soldiers uncovered the Rosetta Stone in the Egyptian desert. Now the stone is displayed in the British Museum in London, England. The Rosetta Stone has been on display since 1802. You can still see it there today.

What story does the Rosetta Stone hold? It was made in 196 B.C. This was nine years after Ptolemy V had been crowned pharaoh, or king. The Rosetta Stone praises Ptolemy. It tells of the good he did for Egypt. But the Rosetta Stone's message had faded into the past. Scholars put time into research and study. They were able to bring this piece of history back to life.

Jean-François Champollion

Glossary

ancient *adj.* of times long past.

link *n.* anything that joins or connects.

scholars *n.* people who have much knowledge.

seeker *n.* one who tries to find; one who searches.

temples *n.* buildings used for worship.

translate *v.* to change from one language into another.

triumph *n.* victory; success.

uncover *v.* to make known; reveal; expose.